WISEBLOOD ESSAYS IN CONTEMPORARY CULTURE No. 7

# THE TRAGEDY OF THE REPUBLIC

PIERRE MANENT

TRANSLATED BY
RALPH C. HANCOCK

WISEBLOOD BOOKS
2024

Third Edition

Copyright © 2024 by Pierre Manent

ISBN: 978-1-963319-83-5

**WISEBLOOD BOOKS**
P.O. Box 870 Menomonee Falls, WI 53052
*www.wisebloodbooks.com*

# PREFACE

The main theme of Pierre Manent's remarkable and important body of work in political theory is the problem of anti-politics as a main aim of modern politics. Beginning with his early studies on liberalism, explorations of the political-theological problem, a fine study on the thought of Alexis de Tocqueville, and continuing through his more recent work in defense of the nation and a reconsideration of natural law, Manent has warned against the modern temptation to empty the public arena of the essential activity of politics.[1] For Manent, politics is the inevitable and inescapable activity for creatures who can neither arrive at exact answers to the complex human condition, nor develop the technological techniques to avoid contentious debate, hard questions, unsatisfying compromise, and uncertain decisions. In sum, we are not creatures who can abandon the effort to discern together the common good.

Nevertheless, a golden thread in modern political thinking and practice has been the effort to eliminate finally the need for politics, either through the temptations of totalitarianism, technocracy, or economism. Manent insists on the perpetual need to develop the virtues of prudence, wisdom, and moderation as the main tools of political engagement. He thus points to the inevitable paradox of this requirement: the conditions necessary to engage in a fruitful and beneficial form of politics arise from the conditions of a well-formed city. Manent has the fortitude to acknowledge that there is no escaping this ancient paradox, but thereby points out that not only have modern thinkers and modern practice insufficiently answered this challenge—they no longer recognize it as a problem.

In this short but rich essay, Manent plumbs this paradox through a comparison of ancient and modern republics. While Manent is a political philosopher, he is concerned with more than merely theoretical questions. As citizens of the world's first explicitly *modern* republic—the United States of America—we are daily faced with this pressing question: why have our leaders so completely failed us? Does the fault lie exclusively in a leadership class that has intentionally disconnected itself from the deepest concerns of the citizenry, meaning that what is therefore needed is an assertion of popular will? Or is the leadership class merely a reflection of the deeper vices today rife throughout the whole of American society, with the only hope lying in some miraculous intervention of an unexpected statesman or a new leadership class that can elevate the national character? Are the people not being adequately represented, or are they altogether too well represented?

Manent makes two claims that are perhaps surprising to the modern reader, but obvious to a thinker steeped in the history of political thought: first, ancient republicanism is an aristocratic form of government; and second, "the great modern political crises can often be described as crises of representation." The modern crisis—as is so often the case—is the result of the very *solution* to the problem in ancient theory and practice. In order to avoid the tricky problem of how best to establish the just rule of a genuine *aristoi* (i.e., "the best"), the architects of modern republicanism proposed representation as a revolutionary advance of the "new science of politics." No longer would republics have to rely upon the existence of a small class of *aristoi*; instead, the people would select leaders based upon their self-interest, and constitutional mechanisms would ensure adequately good rule. If we have a crisis arising from the absence of virtuous leadership *and* public-spirited citizenship today, it is a direct consequence of this modern solution.

Early in the essay, amid a discussion focused on Shakespeare's *Coriolanus*, Manent points to the aristocratic principle of ancient republicanism. He writes, "the spirit of the republic is aristocratic pride, the pride of the few who are 'capable' and 'virtuous'... The life of the republic rests on the emulation of those who judge themselves to be the most capable of governing the city and who expect from the city honors proportionate to their service." Aristocratic emulation, in Manent's reading and in Shakespeare's plays, is a kind of competition among the few that conduces to increased virtue. Accurate as this is, in a republic the people are also encouraged to emulate—that is to say *imitate*—their leaders. More than merely "representing" the people, ancient republicanism insists upon the elevation of the public. The *aristoi* do not merely engage in rule on behalf of the people, but seek to improve the character of the people by encouraging their people to emulate them. In turn, the mechanism by which the people keep the *aristoi* tethered to the common good of the city, and thereby exercise "control" and limit their leaders, is not through elections, but through *honor*. Honor can be withheld, or a leader can be shamed. For an aristocrat, such a fate is worse than being voted out of office, and in this way, motivations relying upon the demands of virtue are reinforced by attention to reputation. The relationship between the many and the few thus relies on two challenging conditions: a leadership class that is genuinely formed by a public-spiritedness formed in virtue and which roots out the shameless and seeks to elevate the populace by stimulating emulation; and a populace which, elevated by a public-spirited ethos, honors (or shames) for right reasons.

Modern republicanism begins with a rejection: we cannot rely upon the presence of such leaders and, in turn, the populace cannot be elevated to such a condition of public-spiritedness. James Madison writes in the justly famous Federalist 10: "It is vain to say that enlightened statesmen will be able to adjust these clashing interests and render them all subservient to the public good. Enlightened statesmen will not always be at the helm."[2] Instead of relying upon *aristoi* to cultivate public-spiritedness, Madison delineates a system that will not merely tolerate but will openly encourage a citizenry who, motivated by private concerns, will form into various factions based upon their interests. They will combine and divide in various ways, coalescing enough to select representatives in large geographic electoral settings. The criteria for the selection of such representatives will be their mere ambi-tion, not their aristocratic virtue; these individuals must be visi-ble enough in larger districts and states to have made a name for themselves. Their ambition will provide the fuel for the eventual checks-and-balances of the Constitutional order, at once animating them through an invisible hand of clashing interests to act on behalf of "the public good," while also limiting their ability to act as tyrants by ensuring adequate competition between offices. Like actors in a market pursuing their interests, almost unwittingly they will behave on behalf of the "public good."

The Constitution's original critics, the so-called "Anti-federalists," anticipated that this mechanism would diminish and corrupt both the people and ruling class: the entire Constitutional system would be riven by private interest. Far from being a *res publica*—concerned with "public things"—modern republicanism would encourage both the elite and the people to see their positions purely in terms of self-interest. The ruling class would seek to use public office—both individually and as a bloc—to enrich themselves, while the governed would come to mistrust and deplore the ruling class. Drawn by ambition to the capital city, a ruling class would develop "courtly habits" and disdain for commoners, with the effect being "above all the perpetual ridicule of virtue."[3] In turn, disillusionment and cynicism toward the political class would prove corrupting to the citizenry. As Melancton Smith (Hamilton's chief opponent in New York) argued during the ratification debates, "government operates upon the spirit of the people, as well as the spirit of the people upon it—and if they are not conformable to each other, the one or the other will prevail."[4] The result is either resignation before the incapacity of politics to resolve this divide, or the very real potential for civil violence and oppression—or both at once: "paralysis and stasis," as Manent warns.

Manent concludes his essay by pointing out that both conditions are the fruition of the "anti-politics" built into modern republicanism. In the absence of self-perpetuating public-spiritedness, our capacity for "emulation and selection" of those who rule "for the common good" withers. The result: "The more the meaning of action withers, the more the capacity to begin and to rule fades away, and the more emulation languishes, the more selection is emptied of meaning." The public will despair that their selection even matters, and the representatives will continue speaking as if they represent, while serving their own interests.

Yet Manent ends on a curiously hopeful note, suggesting that the dénouement of modern republicanism will bring forth its own demise. The "tragedy of the modern republic" is thus not altogether a conclusion to be mourned, he suggests, for from such tragedy might arise the prospect of a new republic and a genuinely post-modern republicanism. The anti-politics of modern representation will ultimately elicit a burst of politics. It may well be that the revival of public-spiritedness will arise not from the bosom of a corrupted leadership class, but from a disquieted demos who will demand public spirit as the price of their selection, and thus take a hand in the shaping of a new *aristoi*.

PATRICK J. DENEEN
*Professor of Political Science*
*David A. Potenziani Memorial College*
*Chair of Constitutional Studies*
*University of Notre Dame*

As the Romans were well aware, the interpretation of signs is a difficult but necessary art.[1] For our part, we neglect the flight of birds, the appetite of sacred chickens, the combat of men in the sky; we have abandoned augury and soothsaying, but we continue to inspect the signs of language. In the words we use, in our choice of them and in their frequency, we seek signs of the movements of our societies and of our souls, the secrets of our aspirations and the key to the future. Of all signs, however, words are the most equivocal, since we use them to articulate what is present, as well as to compensate for or to conjure what is absent. Do the words we use most tell us what we possess or what escapes us? Is the inflation of words a sign of wealth or, on the contrary, of poverty? Our times have witnessed a furor for republicanism and for citizenship. There is no activity so humble that it cannot take on an intimidating nobility as soon as it is associated with citizenship—for example "eating apples" or "sorting recyclables." And the most inconvenient article of swimwear shines with a sinister light as soon as it is declared "contrary to the values of the Republic."[2] The Republic calls us, besieges us, smothers us—but where is the Republic? Are we part of a republic, or does our intemperate usage of the term mean only that we have forgotten its meaning?

I raise these questions seriously, that is to say, in a non-partisan, non-polemical way. I do not mean: our republic is no longer republican enough, and we are no longer citizens, we must try harder! I mean: this collective body that we make up together, is it still legitimate to call it a republic? This question can only be raised seriously if we suspend our participation in the current political debate and strive to grasp "republic" as a discernable and shareable object of thought and subject of action.

To grasp the idea of a republic, not as a marker on a scale of approved opinions, but as a way of life that can be described and evaluated, is not an easy task, for two main reasons. First, as I said, the republican idea seems so near and familiar to us, it envelops us to the point that we experience the effort to hold it at a distance in order to describe and judge it as a kind of impiety; its "value" paralyzes us. Second, we are heirs, or in any case late-comers in a very long history, in the course of which very different political bodies have grown, shone, and declined under the same name of "republic." Thus, how might we, on the one hand, extract ourselves from the grip of the word? And, on the other, how can we avoid losing the real thing by chasing its diverse manifestations?

We are not the first to experience these perplexities, since the question of the republic has never ceased haunting the history of Europe. Throughout this history the most constant reference for giving content to the republican idea has been the Roman republic, just as, symmetrically and inseparably, the Roman Empire provided Europeans with the type for the idea of empire that has occupied their political imagination almost as long. Montaigne provides us with a striking expression of the pregnancy of the republican and Roman idea even in the least favorable circumstances of the republican regime: "I had knowledge of the affairs of Rome long before I knew those of my own house. I knew the Capitol and its layout before I knew the Louvre and the Tiber before the Seine...I engaged in a hundred combats for the defense of Pompey and for Brutus's cause." It would be a mistake to dismiss such weighty testimonies, which could easily be multiplied, as mere anecdotes.

What now limits our *political* interest in the experience of republican Rome—besides, of course, the desire to unsettle scholarly reputations that have in fact already faded—is the well-founded feeling that there is a qualitative difference between ancient and modern republicanism. In fact, since representative government is the great invention of modern politics, what would be the point of seeking useful teachings in an ancient, that is, non-representative republic?

Far be it from me to minimize the importance of the question of political representation. There is no doubt that a good representative regime and a good organization of representation are fundamental conditions of satisfactory political and social life for a modern people. The great modern political crises can often be described as crises of representation. Doubtlessly, many of our contemporary political crises consist to a significant degree in the citizen's loss of confidence in his or her representatives. Nevertheless, even in a representative republic, the basis of political life does not lie in the mechanism of representation. Not only would it be hard to believe in the sincerity of a politician who would say to his fellow citizens: my policy is to represent you; in fact, this would be a sufficient reason not to choose such a person as a representative. Citizens of modern republics choose their representatives in order to be well "represented," to be sure, but also, and first of all, in order to be well *governed*. Representative government has over time been adopted in all European countries and many more besides. This has happened not from love of representation for its own sake, but because in their experience it has seemed to be the best form of government. What, then, is the basis of the representative *republic*, a basis which, again, is not representation, which is only a device, a means to facilitate the good government of large modern societies, with their thousands of responsibilities?

What is the basis of republican government? We hardly ever pose this question; or rather we answer it in a hasty and puerile way, with an answer that is in part double. We say, in effect: the basis of republican government is in principle the pursuit of the general interest but, unfortunately, in practice it is most often particular interests that prevail. Equipped with this important information, we citizens are full of admiration for our good intentions and pitilessly severe towards the politicians who, of course, betray them. How might we avoid this mix of moralism and skepticism that makes us both idle and querulous as citizens?

For once we must think not of ourselves, but of those who govern us. What is the basis of their action? We must not by any means ask them, since they will repeat the platitudes called for by the representative system, which we do not believe anyway. Whom to ask, then? The advantage of the non-representative republic, especially the Roman republic, is that it makes available to us the spirit and motives of republican government, which are here more visible because they are not veiled or distorted by the enormous artifice of representation. Without necessarily following Montaigne in "taking up the fight" for Pompey or Brutus, we would thus be well advised, in order to know precisely where we stand, to interrogate the Romans.

To interrogate the Romans, I propose to interrogate Shakespeare. Since this approach does not go without saying, I owe the reader a brief explanation. Shakespeare's Roman plays follow faithfully Plutarch's *Parallel Lives*, making the exceptions to this rule especially instructive. Plutarch was a historian and philosopher admired by Montaigne and Rousseau for his particularly acute judgment of human actions and for his skill in revealing the bases of these actions. The drama of the theatre, moreover, is all about action: on the stage, all speech serves action or is bound up with it, thus bringing to the surface, by its very form, the springs of human action, revealing why human beings do what they do. Shakespeare's Roman plays thus make available to us, not of course an "historical document," but an interrogation or inquiry into the motives of the actors of that republican regime which left the deepest mark on the history of Europe and of the West. This is where we will look for the bases of the republic, that is, for the typical motives of actors in this form of common life.

There are three of Shakespeare's Roman plays that are pertinent to our discussion: *Coriolanus*, *Julius Caesar*, and *Antony and*

*Cleopatra*. Considered together, they form an exhaustive dramatic exploration of the political arc of Rome. *Coriolanus* is the most completely political play; it is exclusively and one might say obsessively political: the city is the beginning and the end of all the actions of all the characters. In contrast with the civic closure of *Coriolanus*, *Antony and Cleopatra* deals only with the "world," the division or unity of the world; there is even, beginning in the first lines, the question of finding out a "new heaven, a new earth." The aging *Imperator* and the sorceress of the Nile seek to fill, by their passion alone, a world that is henceforth both without a city and deserted by the city's gods. Between these two, there is the brevity and concentrated sparseness of *Julius Caesar*. Unlike *Coriolanus*, where human motives are in a way produced and inscribed by the authority of the city, in *Julius Caesar* the motives of at least some of the main characters are infected with uncertainty and ambiguity, and the double rupture of the republican compact, first by Caesar's tyranny and then by his murder, leaves Brutus and Cassius (the last Romans worthy of the name) incapable of either acting effectively together or re-gathering the Roman people and thus re-unifying the disjointed pieces of their humanity. Regretfully setting aside *Antony and Cleopatra*, our inquiry will limit itself to the two other tragedies.[3]

We must, of course, begin with *Coriolanus*. I will not attempt to summarize the play, but I would just like to point out several of the main teachings of this tragedy considered as a political drama. The first is especially disagreeable and bitter for us, but for this reason it is particularly useful. I will formulate it thus: the principle of the republic is aristocratic; the spirit of those who govern a republic is aristocratic pride, the pride of the few who are "capable" and "virtuous." Coriolanus takes this pride to the point of insolence and furor, but it is the general principle of the regime. The life of the republic rests on the emulation of those who judge themselves to be the most capable of governing the city and who expect from the city honors proportionate to their service. This aristocratic character is not limited to the beginnings of the republic, which would then "necessarily" come into its own by adopting the democratic regime. It belongs to the essence of a self-governing political body, one that by its very nature wishes to be governed by the best. We spontaneously identify republicanism with equality, because our republic was formed on the basis of citizens equalized by absolute monarchy against the residues of an aristocracy of privileges that no longer performed any political function. Moreover, relying on the consent of the many, the modern device of representation is designed to artificially manufacture a few who are "capable," though not necessarily "virtuous."

What characterizes Coriolanus—Shakespeare's in any case, since Plutarch's is more conciliatory—is not that he refuses to concede anything to the people. The people, he says, know neither how to make war nor how to live in peace; they cannot govern and do not want to be governed. Thus, named consul by the Senate as a reward for his exploits, he finds it very difficult to conform to the convention of the regime, which requires that the designated consul ask for the support and voices of the people. Coriolanus finally manages to bend to the custom, all the while covering the plebeians with sarcasm, even though they give him their voices and acclaim him the new consul. Stirred up by the tribunes, the plebeians soon repent of their vote. In a great political scene populated by senators and the people's tribunes, Coriolanus offers a ferocious and brilliant critique of the divided character of Roman government and demands that the tribunes of the plebs—an office only recently established—be reversed. In response, the tribunes accuse him of "manifest treason" and condemn this proud man to death.

As I mentioned in passing, Plutarch's Coriolanus is less implacable: contrary to Shakespeare's character, he willingly shows his wounds to the people. Thus Shakespeare takes the dominant nature of Coriolanus, his aristocratic pride, to the extreme, and so brings out the contradiction inherent in this pride, which causes him to covet the honors that he despises because he despises those who grant them. Whether it is a question of asking for the voices of the plebeians or of showing his wounds, Coriolanus finds the process repugnant because it injures his independence and implies that his virtues are not sufficient in themselves, but require the people's confirmation. When Coriolanus asks a citizen what price he must pay the people for the position of consul, the citizen answers: "The price is to ask it kindly" (II.iii. 83–84). Coriolanus ("Kindly!") considers this an exorbitant price!

For Shakespeare's Coriolanus, for whom action and even great feats are easy, speech is the occasion of continual torment. He demands that his action suffice to itself and that he thus should have no obligation to accompany it with words, even as a matter of simple courtesy. This is what is not possible in a republic. And so, words are always throwing him off course. Too sensitive to the words of others, which easily make him furious, he is incapable of mastering his own, which tend naturally to condescension and sarcasm. He can hardly bear to be complimented. He is incapable of speaking humanely or calmly to members of the popular class. "You speak o' the people, as if you were a god to punish, not a man of their infirmity," a tribune tells him (III.i.80–83). Acts of war, in which he excels and exults, are speechless. His general, Cominius, relating the great deeds and valor of Coriolanus, describes him as "a thing of blood, whose every motion was timed with dying cries" (II.ii. 107–8).

Shakespeare, in the character of Coriolanus, takes to the maximum degree the figure of the great citizen whose action, because it evidently and eminently serves the city, wishes to be independent of the approval of citizens and possess within itself the worth it deserves. In any case, what pertinent dialogue could there be between a ruler responsible for everything and everyone and the numberless ruled, each of whom sees but a tiny part of the common concern? Yet this is the supremely unequal dialogue that the great citizen, a Lincoln or a De Gaulle, must know how to elicit and to conduct. The test of the republic lies in the almost impossible task of joining speech to deed and deed to speech, each to each aptly and justly. To speak is easy, and to act is hard; but nothing is harder than to act while initiating, accompanying, and completing action by the appropriate words; consider the rarity and brevity of the Appeal of June 18th or the Gettysburg Address. The republic, in its principle and in its health, is on the side of action that, if not wholly unaccompanied by speech, at least employs words very sparingly.

In Shakespeare's *Coriolanus*, a citizen provides the formula for a just exchange between ruler and citizens: "if he show us his wounds and tell us his deeds, we are to put our tongues into those wounds and speak for them" (II.iii.5–7). The evocation is not the most pleasant, but it defines very precisely how, in a well-constituted republic, the mute eloquence of wounds—assuming the hero is willing to show them—meets the speech of citizens who "speak for them." As readers of Shakespeare well know, this strange image of wounds that speak is also found in *Julius Caesar*, precisely in the decisive episode of the tragedy, since it concerns Antony's speech, those fateful words which will cause the people's opinion to swing against Caesar's murderers. We must comment on this famous passage, since it vividly traces a crucial transformation: the fundamentally healthy republic of Coriolanus into the painfully corrupt republic of Caesar.

Antony is a friend and a partisan of Caesar. (As we will discuss further, he was imprudently spared by the conspirators.) He has just presented him the crown three times, which Caesar has three times refused. With Brutus's authorization, Antony eulogizes Caesar before the people. Antony's speech is a drama within the tragedy. It is very long; one hears reactions from the audience; Antony transforms the forum into the stage of a theatre; using every actor's trick—he takes a long break to cry, for example—and having no use for argument appealing to reason or the common good, he intends to act only on the most elementary emotions of the people, mainly soliciting compassion for Caesar, whose body is exposed to everyone's view, and appeals to the people's own interests, at least the interests of the people such as Antony presents them. In *Coriolanus* the people, whether hesitant or fickle, are a political people, speaking and acting with a vivid awareness of political stakes, especially constitutional stakes. The people who are listening to Antony are at a show, experiencing emotions, and, although they turn finally against Caesar's murderers, they enter into no active relation to his situation. Instead, what is decisive for them is the fact that Caesar has bequeathed them his private gardens and newly planted orchards as well as seventy-five drachmas for each person. Antony does not fail to enunciate: for each person!

Let us come to the passage that holds special interest for us. Even though he has already been speaking a long time, Antony declares abruptly that he is not an orator, that he has neither wit, nor words, nor worth, nor action, nor utterance, nor the power of speech: "[I] show you sweet Caesar's wounds, poor poor dumb mouths, and bid them speak for me." But, he continues, if he were an orator, he would "put a tongue in every wound of Caesar that should move the stones of Rome to rise and mutiny" (III.ii.222–7).[4] In this spectacular moment nothing remains of the civic relation between the wounds of the living hero Coriolanus and people: the plebeians desired to render him justice, and to maintain their place in the republican order precisely by rendering this justice. All that remains is the ever more brilliant speech of the orator, who does not know how to speak to his fellow citizens because he is no longer appealing to them *as* citizens. Nonetheless, Antony would know how to give eloquence to the mute wounds of the dead hero, wounds that might bring the stones of Rome to life.

This prodigious piece of rhetoric seals the end of Roman civic and political eloquence, the eloquence of Cicero, whom, notably,

Shakespeare never has speak in the tragedy and who will soon die a victim of Antony's vengeance. Public speech is henceforth severed from any significant relation to action. At the same time, the success of Antony's eloquence is not without a certain power of political revelation: what remains of collective attention in Rome is concentrated on Caesar's pierced body and on his flowing blood. In the body and the blood of Caesar now resides the greatest power.

Whereas the republican regime was founded on the most intense and constant possible mobilization of man's *active* faculties, the new regime will derive its strange force from the authority of a prince who has been assassinated and reduced to the ultimate passivity of death. Since Shakespeare was writing in a Christian age, his fixed attention on Caesar's body and blood forces us to recall the body and blood of Christ. What are we to make of such an explicit parallelism? Is Shakespeare suggesting a political interpretation of Christianity, in which Caesar, by his finally vanquished strength, produces the collective form that will soon be inhabited by the finally victorious weakness of Christ? I do not know. If we do not look beyond the political order, we would say that Caesar, by the audacity and the height of his ascension as well as by the shocking contingency of his fall, had left an imprint large and deep enough to clothe opposed souls with the same authority: princes who fear losing their power find solace in his broken body, and those who aspire to seize that same power find in his blood the boldness to seize it.

It is time to consider the other party, the party of Caesar's murderers, and especially Brutus, whom many good readers find to be the main and most interesting character of the tragedy—even to the point that it should bear his name. I will continue to follow the same thread, that of the relation between speech and action.

Brutus's speech before the people of Rome, in which he justifies his action, is—stylistically—the complete opposite of Antony's. It is, I want to say, brutally rational, and is built upon very abrupt antitheses and contrasts: I honor Caesar for his valor; I killed him for his ambition. I loved Caesar, but I loved Rome still more. It is above all extremely brief, which presupposes that the listeners will be instantaneously persuaded, even as this juxtaposition of propositions does not appear to an ordinary understanding to be easily compatible. In short, Brutus's rhetoric as a whole presupposes that the goodness of his cause is evident, and that it is enough for him to declare it in order to persuade everyone. This disposition, which is so distinctive of Brutus, constitutes at once his greatness and his weakness. And to say it directly at the outset: he justifies his action in mediocre fashion for the same reason that this action has been very clumsily conducted. We must not overestimate Brutus.

It is not Brutus, but Cassius, who initiates the conspiracy. This friend and relative of Brutus is an excellent judge of men and of situations. We can say with confidence: if he had led the conspiracy alone, it would have taken another turn altogether and the death of Caesar might have opened up a completely different history; the conspirators might have been able to renovate the Roman republic by giving it a form that it is impossible for us to imagine. More precisely: Cassius cannot act without Brutus, for he needs, first of all, Brutus's credibility, in order to recruit the others in the group and give them confidence in the enterprise, and, once the deed is done, to persuade the people—or so he hopes—of its legitimacy. Once he has persuaded Brutus to join the conspiracy, Brutus, by his eminence, necessarily becomes its head and leads it as he sees fit.

Brutus is admired by all for his virtue. He is by unanimous consent the most virtuous Roman.[5] An enterprise takes on a different color when he takes part in it. We have no reason to think that this moral reputation is not deserved. The question is whether Brutus's disinterestedness—admirable in itself—is the best disposition for leading an action of such consequence and gravity.

Cassius, for his part, is anything but disinterested. He has seen Caesar, his old companion in war and in play, whom he once saved from drowning during a storm, and whose physical weaknesses he knows well—he has seen this man, who was not more a man than he, Cassius, become a god, while he himself has been reduced to waiting for Caesar to deign to look upon him. There is no doubt that resentment and envy rule his actions. At the same time, we cannot consider him a resentful person or one ruled by envy, because his admiring friendship for Brutus is both sincere and lucid to an astonishing degree. The question would be rather: does Cassius's burning resentment, which provides him with such a powerful motive for action, deprive this action of its moral and political legitimacy? After all, what is wrong with experiencing Caesar's exorbitant power over Rome as a personal humiliation? What is wrong with hating the tyrant as well as the tyranny? Is Cassius's personal hatred for Caesar more immoral than the special friendship that Brutus maintains for Caesar, even though he is oppressing the "generality" of the very Romans Brutus says are his only concern?

In any case, having agreed to participate in the conspiracy, and having immediately and naturally taken over its leadership, Brutus rejects three proposals of Cassius that seemed particularly judicious. The most significant is the third: would it not be prudent to kill Antony, a skillful intriguer disposing of powerful means, along with Caesar? Brutus refuses this expedient: such an action would appear too bloody; we must circumscribe the deed as much as possible in order to show that the murderers acted not by envious passion but according to strict necessity. Strangely, Brutus, rather than seriously discussing the harm that Antony might do and the risk that the conspirators would be taking in allowing him to live, is interested only in the appearance of such an action, and in the impression that it would make, one is tempted to say, on an impartial spectator. Brutus seems to be as much preoccupied by the appearance of an action's morality as by the morality itself, not to mention its effectiveness. Stranger still, in order to dismiss

Cassius's suggestion, he suddenly changes registers: "Let us be sacrificers, but not butchers, Caius." He thus situates their action in a religious register, or in any case a register superior to human deliberation. Rather than seriously considering the best way to conduct their action, Brutus reinterprets it and strives to cancel it out imaginatively. He continues in this way:

> We all stand up against the spirit of Caesar;
> And in the spirit of men there is no blood:
> O, that we then could come by Caesar's spirit,
> And not dismember Caesar! But, alas,
> Caesar must bleed for it! And, gentle friends,
> Let's kill him boldly, but not wrathfully;
> Let's carve him as a dish fit for the gods,
> Not hew him as a carcass fit for hounds. (II.i.165–173)

It should be noted that Brutus does not hesitate; he does not reconsider his resolve to kill Caesar; he is even the most undaunted of the conspirators, reinforcing the dispositions of Cassius himself when he begins to flinch. As I was saying, he reinterprets the action before it begins; he makes of the deed something other than what it had seemed it must be; he cancels it out imaginatively as a human and political action. He depoliticizes and thereby "derepublicanizes" the great action that has been decided upon. The political and moral situation as Cassius had described it so vividly and concretely is no longer recognizable. It is no longer a matter of a man who has become a tyrant and a god because of the Romans' cowardice. It is a question of a being who is neither man nor god, but spirit and blood, and the conspirators, or rather the sacrificers, will not be *killing* either a man or a tyrant, but will be *separating* Caesar's spirit from his blood. Brutus explains that in order to reach Caesar's spirit they have no other choice but to spill his blood. This fiction, which reveals an imaginative turn one might find unpleasant, nevertheless contains and announces the coming reality. Caesar's spirit, liberated from its ties to Caesar's blood, will prolong and extend the tyrant's power. After Cassius's death, just before his own, Brutus will cry out:

> O Julius Caesar, thou art mighty yet!
> Thy spirit walks abroad and turns our swords
> In our own proper entrails. (V.iii.94–96)

Let us try to gather the threads of the drama. The action would never have begun without the passion, the energy, and the judgment of Cassius. And Cassius would never have been able to complete the deed without the participation and the credibility of Brutus, who by his eminence will alone decide the way to proceed. Brutus contributes decisively to the success of the conspiracy, at least in its first phase, by his unshakeable confidence. He is the most scrupulous, and at the same time the one who trembles least. This is first of all because of his complete confidence in the goodness of the cause. It is also and inseparably because he isolates himself from accidents and circumstances by means of a mainly moral perception of things. Certain of doing good, Brutus neglects to do it well. Cassius, inversely, because of both his unfettered judiciousness and his anxious attention to circumstances, tends to lack confidence in himself and in the cause.[6] Excess confidence on the one hand and excess doubt on the other conspire to the common defeat.

It is reasonable to think that they would have won the victory if Cassius had sometimes resisted Brutus's authority, or if Brutus had deferred to Cassius's prudence. The tragedy resides in the fact that neither the eminent personal qualities of these two great citizens, nor their close and sincere friendship, nor the greatness and the urgency of the stakes, were able to bring them to make a truly common decision following a truly common deliberation. A rift was always opening up between them. Its cause lay in Brutus's superiority, in the influence he could not put aside and from which Cassius never wished to or never was able to free himself. This is piercingly clear in the saddest, most bitter, and most beautiful scene of the tragedy, when, in the midst of a very violent quarrel, Brutus's bad faith pushes Cassius's wounded friendship to despair. Having invited Brutus to stab him as he had stabbed Caesar, Cassius cries out:

> ... for, I know,
> When thou didst hate him worst, thou lovedst him better
> Than ever thou lovedst Cassius. (IV.ii.155–157)

Brutus gives no answer, but this ray of cruel truth immediately deflates his unjust anger, and the friendship is renewed, even if the fissure is never overcome.

Cassius has put his finger on the painful point. The closest, most sincere, and noblest friendship cannot abolish inequality, nor remove its sting. Cassius's cry demands that we reconsider the tragedy's architecture. It is of course an account of the republican conspiracy, the conspiracy of the good party, against the tyrant Caesar, and of the ruinous consequences for this same party. This conspiracy rests on the ambivalent figure of Brutus. He is the leader, first implicit and then explicit, of the republican party. Must it be said that this position contradicts his status as a special friend of Caesar? This is indeed the case, as long as we add that he shares with Caesar, besides the bond of personal friendship, the complicity of superiority. Brutus alone is comparable—or potentially comparable—with Caesar. He alone, we might say today, is in Caesar's category. Note that the plebeians, who understood nothing of Brutus's speech in the forum, but who sensed something important, cry out at the end of the speech: "Let him be Caesar." And again: "Caesar's better parts shall be crown'd in Brutus." (III.ii.50–51)

Brutus is not inclined to tyranny. He is, in fact, a good republican and would never become another Caesar. And yet, what is to be done with his superiority, which brings him Caesar's friendship and esteem, as well as the trust of the republican conspirators? By fleeing towards the "general" and that which is held in "common," he avoids considering his personal position. He does not lay down his superiority, since he exercises his influence over Cassius himself without the least reticence, but wraps it in an exclusive concern for "the common," in which every person's position, beginning with his own, becomes invisible. He is the most virtuous of Romans, but possesses the least self-knowledge—or knows least what he is doing. He does not manage to discern or produce action or conduct to match his capacities and deserts under the conditions determined by Caesar's exorbitant power. He can neither ally himself with Caesar, nor prepare himself to succeed him, nor kill him in a useful way.

This political and moral analysis is obviously too rough, but it is sufficient to indicate the reasons for my perplexity concerning the mimetic interpretation of the tragedy proposed by René Girard. The core of Girard's thesis, and for me the stumbling block, is given in the characterization of Cassius as the "mediator of hate."[7] I find the expression abstract, that is, apolitical. It neglects or rather dismisses the concrete reality of the action. Cassius is first of all *the one who begins*, who takes the initiative, who is pushed by no one, but pushes all the others. René Girard discerns well that Cassius is the "true father" of the conspiracy, but he does not duly consider either the initial action or the arch-actor who must persuade the other potential actors to join him. The fact that he is particularly envious of Caesar is an anecdotal factor in comparison with this: Cassius initiates the action. This is the feature that matters politically. The term "hate," employed by Girard, is otherwise perfectly adequate. There is no doubt that Cassius hates Caesar. But this word "hate" is so politically, and thus morally, imprecise! Unless we think that all hatreds are alike, that all hate is the same hate, that is, the same sin— and this may indeed be Girard's view— we will be led to distinguish between hatreds, between the qualities that hatred can take on. In any case I will go so far as to say that there are noble and base hatreds. A very honorable political and moral tradition, one, I must emphasize, that is Christian as well as pagan, holds that hatred for the tyrant is a noble hatred, and that it belongs to the virtue of the good citizen. We might make all we can of the role of personal resentment in Cassius's hatred (which in any case he does not let us ignore); we can say that Caesar's tyrannical character is a matter of debate; but we cannot entirely pass over the meaning the actors give to their action or overlook the fact that the person who is the object of hatred is considered to be a tyrant by an important part of the most competent and honorable citizens. If we neglect this fact we will be obliged to say, or at least to think, that hatred has settled on Caesar *by chance.*

It would be a mistake to confuse the crystallization of the conspiracy with the contagion of hatred. Hatred is not contagious like an infectious disease. Cassius, moreover, does not awaken the hatred of the conspirators who, with the exception of Brutus, already hate Caesar; he convinces them to act according to their hatred, which is something different, and which requires something besides hatred. In any case, Brutus, who will take the lead in the conspiracy, does not hate and will never hate Caesar. It is impossible to say why Brutus decides to participate in the action. One thing alone is clear: as tormented as he is before the decision, he is no less implacably resolute once it is taken. As I have emphasized, it is Brutus who knows himself the least. He is of course perfectly aware that the reason he cannot sleep is that Cassius "did whet" him "against Caesar" (II.i.64). But he was troubled long before Cassius's devices. Again, Cassius does not awaken Brutus's hatred for Caesar, but sets off the desire to participate in the plot. How is that?

According to Cassius—who, I remind you, is by Caesar's own admission an excellent observer of men and their actions—what is important for Brutus is the high opinion of him in Rome, the greatness of his "name." Cassius holds a mirror up to Brutus: he must see himself as Rome sees him. His "name" fills Rome as much as Caesar's does. His name fills Rome and Rome fills his soul. Caesar no longer really exists. So Brutus, like a logician who cannot be stopped, will soon distinguish the real Caesar that he continues to love from the possible Caesar that he is resolved to kill. I do not think that one clarifies anything by making Caesar "an insurmountable obstacle, the *skandalon* of mimetic rivalry."[8] This leaves out the third term, which is Rome, the common thing. Rome comes between Brutus and his friends. Brutus loves Cassius, but despises him because he is too human. He loves Caesar still more, but he kills him because he might become inhuman. He wants to have no moral relation except with what he calls the "general." What opposes certain insurmountable "frictions" to the mechanism singled out by the mimetic theory is the "common," the enlargement of the soul that is implied in membership in the republic, the unequal enlargement of souls that nourishes in some a legitimate and supremely dangerous pride. The great citizen is not only greater or smaller than another great citizen, he is also and first of all greater than himself, for he has another body and another soul, that of Rome. This enlargement is bearable or controllable only when everyone acts under the view, not of all, but of the common, of the Republic, and with respect for its laws and institutions, as difficult as this may be, as the example of Coriolanus attests. Caesar's disproportionate ascent, so well diagnosed by Cassius, has rendered impossible this arbitration by means of "the common." Since the real and effective "common" has withered, Brutus allows himself to be carried away by an imagined "common" in whose name he sacrifices a Caesar he himself has declared to be imaginary. His hand does not tremble, because, rather than carrying out a terrible action, he is presiding over a rite of his own invention.

There are two great modalities of the acting human being, that of the one who begins and that of the one who commands. Caesar was both. Cassius was one, Brutus the other. The republic, "the common," allows, not everyone, but the few "virtuous" to be both initiators and rulers as long as they obey its laws. The republic allows for much action; it encourages much action, because it mobilizes the most powerful spring of action, which is emulation among equals. The republic is the regime that allows and encourages the most action. This can be seen in Rome, and we see it in England in the seventeenth and eighteenth centuries, a "republic disguised under the form of monarchy."[9] We see it in America's founding, an extraordinary founding, and we see it in France in the great movement of '89, especially if this movement is understood to include, as it ought, the adventure of the Empire.

Today we expect from a republic the opposite of a republic. We demand from it the least possible action, or what we call "freedom." For us, freedom is a world without commandment or obedience, especially a world in which public action can neither begin nor command anything. In practice, as I have noted, we ask our representatives and those who govern us to show their disinterestedness in defending our interests. In this we give evidence of a very naïve immorality, but especially we use a moralizing language that prevents us from grasping the moral bases of a truly republican regime. Service to the republic cannot be disinterested because it is paid for by what is most precious in the eyes of ambitious citizens, that is, the honor granted by the Republic, public esteem being the first and finally the only one. It is definitely not disinterestedness that we should be asking of those who govern us, but rather ambition. It has been so long since we had the rare benefit of being governed by a truly ambitious statesman. The conviction has taken hold that our regime would be more republican if it ignored political rule still more. This is to turn our backs on the republic. The reigning social philosophy postulates the power and self-sufficiency of a spontaneous social order that would bring together order and freedom without the mediation of political rule. This is to abandon society to its inertia, that is, its corruption. Thus, places and states of toxic stagnation have formed, spreading and producing cysts on the social body over the last few decades; these places have never known the presence of political rule.

As I have said, the basis of the republic is pride in ruling for the common good, and thus the emulation and selection of those who are the most capable, which is never a large number. The more the meaning of action withers, the more the capacity to begin and to rule fades away, and the more emulation languishes, the more selection is emptied of meaning. When one opens the polls to decide who will have the honor of not acting, rivalries can be lively and passions virulent, but the men and women who fear ruling all look alike. Paralysis and stasis are taking hold and sinking roots, with the fervent help of citizens who demand action and protest successfully at the first sign of it. Where might we find action that begins and commands? I do not know. But European man, so long known for action, cannot flee indefinitely. European humanity cannot live indefinitely without any form. There are among us both reasonable citizens and passionate citizens who are waiting for the event that would force us to give ourselves some form, a European form for some and a national form for others. All discern the proliferation of signs telling our fate, which they interpret in opposite ways. Is not this tension without any plausible resolution the beginning of tragedy, of the tragedy of the modern republic? Is this not our tragedy?

# NOTES

## PREFACE

1. See, for instance, these books by Pierre Manent: *An Intellectual History of Liberalism*, translated by Rebecca Balinski (Princeton: Princeton University Press, 1994); *Tocqueville and the Nature of Democracy*, translated by John Waggoner (Lanham, MD: Rowman & Littlefield Publishers, 1996); *The City of Man*, translated by Marc A. LePain (Princeton: Princeton University Press, 1998); *A World Beyond Politics?*, translated by Marc A. LePain (Princeton: Princeton University Press, 2006); *Metamorphoses of the City: On the Western Dynamic*, translated by Mark A. LePain (Cambridge, MA: Harvard University Press, 2013); *Natural Law and Human Rights: Toward a Recovery of Practical Reason*, translated by Ralph C. Hancock (South Bend, IN: University of Notre Dame Press, 2020).

2. James Madison, *Federalist 10*; in James Madison, Alexander Hamilton, John Jay, *The Federalist Papers*, edited by Isaac Kramnick (New York: Penguin Books, 1987 [1788]), 125.

3. Cato, Letter IV; in Herbert Storing, *What the Anti-Federalists Were For* (Chicago: University of Chicago Press, 1981), 20.

4. Melancton Smith, in Storing, *(op. cit),* 19.

## THE TRAGEDY OF THE REPUBLIC

1. Consider Cassius, who in *Julius Caesar,* awed by such signs, says to Casca:

> You look pale and gaze
> And put on fear and cast yourself in wonder,
> To see the strange impatience of the heavens:
> But if you would consider the true cause
> Why all these fires, why all these gliding ghosts,
> Why birds and beasts from quality and kind,
> Why old men fool and children calculate,
> Why all these things change from their ordinance
> Their natures and preformed faculties
> To monstrous quality—why, you shall find
> That heaven hath infused them with these spirits,
> To make them instruments of fear and warning
> Unto some monstrous state.

> Now could I, Casca, name to thee a man
> Most like this dreadful night,
> That thunders, lightens, opens graves, and roars
> As doth the lion in the Capitol,
> A man no mightier than thyself or me
> In personal action, yet prodigious grown
> And fearful, as these strange eruptions are (I.iii.62–81).

2. Manent here alludes to the "burkini controversy" in France, wherein wearing of the burkini was banned by a number of French municipalities.

3. Manent means to indicate that *Antony and Cleopatra* is a play about the whole world, rather than a play concerning a limited set of political actors dealing with a specific civic problem (the problem of the "city"). It is in the broadest sense a "political" play, but not in the same way as the other two. In *Metamorphoses of the City* Manent writes at length about the relationship between city and empire:

> Rome's uniqueness resides not only in the fact that under the same name it prospered, first as warrior republic and then as an immense empire, but also that the latter came out of the former. The self-destruction of the republican city was in a certain sense the cause of the empire coming into existence… The fact that only in Rome was extreme corruption not fatal means that Rome is a phenomenon that contradicts not only the ontology of politics, as I have already said, but even ontology *tout court*. In Rome death was not deadly… If the transformation or metaphor of city into empire is at the center of the "Roman Question," then that question comes together or is summed up in the figure of Julius Caesar—who became more, and something other, than a Roman citizen, as eminent and glorious as one imagines him, yet without however seizing the royal crown that was offered him and that he apparently coveted so much. In "missing" the royal crown, he founded a new kind of monarchy, not only because he was the true founder of the Roman Empire, but also because he gave his name to an unprecedented phenomenon, "Caesarism." What is Caesarism? It is a monarchy that follows a republic no longer able to govern itself (117).

4. Antony is even "sincere." A little earlier, kneeling before Caesar's body, he had cried: "Over thy wounds now do I prophesy (Which like dumb mouths do ope their ruby lips To beg the voice and utterance of my tongue), A curse shall light upon the limbs of men… " (III.i. 260–3).

5. After his death, Antony himself will declare this:

> This was the noblest Roman of them all:
> All the conspirators save only he
> Did that they did in envy of great Caesar;
> He only, in a general honest thought
> And common good to all, made one of them.
> His life was gentle, and the elements
> So mixed in him that Nature might stand up
> And say to all the world 'This was a man!'
> (V.v.68–75)

6. "Mistrust of good success hath done this deed." (V.iii.66)

7. See René Girard, *Shakespeare les feux de l'envie*, tr. B. Vincent, Grasset, 1990, p. 233\*\*

8. Ibid., p. 235.

9. Montesquieu, *The Spirit of the Laws*, V.19.

**PIERRE MANENT** is professor emeritus of political philosophy at the École des Hautes Études en Sciences Sociales. He is the author of numerous books, including *Tocqueville and the Nature of Democracy, The City of Man, A World Beyond Politics?, Metamorphoses of the City: On the Western Dynamic*, and *Natural Law and Human Rights: Toward a Recovery of Practical Reason*.

**PATRICK J. DENEEN** is professor of political science and holds the David A. Potenziani Memorial College Chair of Constitutional Studies at the University of Notre Dame. His books include *The Odyssey of Political Theory, Democratic Faith*, and *Why Liberalism Failed*.

*Translated by Ralph C. Hancock*

Wiseblood Essays in Contemporary Culture
champion and criticize strands of Catholic culture,
and critique and interpret culture at large
from a broadly Catholic vantage point.

The Catholic Writer Today
*Dana Gioia · No. 1*

The Catholic Imagination in Modern American Poetry
*James Matthew Wilson · No. 2*

The Lost World:
American Catholic Non-Fiction at Midcentury
*Kevin Starr · No. 3*

"Everything Came to Me at Once":
The Intellectual Vision of René Girard
*Cynthia L. Haven · No. 4*

How to Think Like a Poet
*Ryan Wilson · No. 5*

Duty, the Soul of Beauty:
Henry James on the Beautiful Life
*R.R. Reno · No. 6*

www.ingramcontent.com/pod-product-compliance
Lightning Source LLC
LaVergne TN
LVHW020930290725
817333LV00008B/440